Margaret was diagnosed with ovarian cancer, the "silent killer", in October 2016; she was told to prepare for death.

She set about using her passion for words to write her poetry over the remaining two years of her life. She died in October 2018.

Margaret used her passion to compose, and together with her desire to articulate her feelings, has left a body of work which is meant to move the reader and to give hope.

Each poem sets out the anguish of suffering but lifts the reader because of the love set out in her compositions, and they portray Margaret's tenacity, gratitude for the love given to her, her intelligence and the belief Margaret had that she would be released from pain as she ascended into eternal peace.

Margaret said to me, "I am writing something for you; read it when I am gone", when I did read her work, my heart ached with pain, my tears fell, and I screamed in anguish.

Margaret wanted to dedicate her work to her family, who she adored, The Christie Hospital and all their wonderful staff and, of course, all the people at the Maggie Centre who inspired and provided support throughout her desire to leave a written legacy.

Margaret Ffrench

NOTES FROM THE HEART, WHISPERS OF THE SOUL

Light, Love and
Reflections on the Infinite

AUSTIN MACAULEY PUBLISHERS™
LONDON * CAMBRIDGE * NEW YORK * SHARJAH

Copyright © Margaret Ffrench 2024

The right of Margaret Ffrench to be identified as the author of this work has been asserted by the author in accordance with sections 77 and 78 of the Copyright, Designs and Patents Act 1988.

All rights reserved. No part of this publication may be reproduced, stored in a retrieval system, or transmitted in any form or by any means, electronic, mechanical, photocopying, recording, or otherwise, without the prior permission of the publishers.

Any person who commits any unauthorised act in relation to this publication may be liable to criminal prosecution and civil claims for damages.

A CIP catalogue record for this title is available from the British Library.

ISBN 9781035830046 (Paperback)
ISBN 9781035830053 (Hardback)
ISBN 9781035830060 (ePub e-book)

www.austinmacauley.co.uk

First Published 2024
Austin Macauley Publishers Ltd®
1 Canada Square
Canary Wharf
London
E14 5AA

My sincere thanks to all the good people at AM Publishers who have seen the gift that Margaret had to move people with her compositions and have the belief in her work to support its publication.

I want to write a poem

I scrape the letter off the floor and walls
And toss them, dice like, onto the white page
Where they bristle, spiky and black.
I try to mould them into something of beauty.
But they resist.
Disobedient, unruly, ugly.
Like flattened spiders, splattered.
Where I wanted pressed flowers
Like hieroglyphics they make no sense to me.
The creep away, slip skidding out of the corner of my eye.

Here is my life

Here is my life
Laid out before you
Unfurled like a carpet roll.
A patchwork of jewelled colours
Like the wings of the dragonfly
Intricate,
Intense.
Here are my babies
Blood of our blood
And here is my wedding ring
A symbol of eternity
Here, here and here
All my tears.
These are my heartaches
And these intricate stitches
In glorious incandescent colours.
These are my joys
This frayed, ragged edge
This ending
This is the full stop.

Life is a little silver bird
I catch it in hand
In my Palms
Fingers circling
I feel its fragility
Its heart beat
But it won't stay
Like water, like sand on the holiday beach
It slips through my grasp.
I love you my love, we say to each other.
We weep / my bald head stroked by you
Always have, always will.
How can I reassure you?
How tell you I won't be gone. I won't leave you.
How promise what I don't know
This I can say –
That feather,
That soft breeze,
The rocking chair gently rocking,
The cat suddenly staring
This I promise – if I can I will. Think it is me and be comforted.
When you go, too go I hold my hand out to you.

After

My time has come
My soul needs to be released from the prison of my body.
With a gasp, my soul bursts free.
A shape shifting, undulating bubble
Sheens of oil-like colours shivering over the surface.
Undeniable yearning urges my soul on.
The trajectory arrow wise following an unstoppable force
Thrusting onward.
A million hands
Tiny, large, small
Propel my soul on
Pushing, pulling, caressing, encouraging.
A murmur of voices all around
Whispering, singing
All different
Swelling into a crescendo of rejoicing.
Echoes of known voicing,
Glimpses of familiar faces
Memories flash
Light pulsating like oil on water.

And so my soul enters in God.
God's great reservoir of love takes me in.
As the singing swells and surges
I realise that my soul is singing too
I am known
I am welcomed.
All pain, sorrow, sadness, washed away.
Gone.
I am being absorbed.
She absorbs me into Herself.
I am no longer I
But we, us.
Happiness flows through me.
Joyful peace.
A wonderful eternity.
It is beautiful
Beautiful
Beautiful.

Burial

Not for me no slate grey, thunder dark Cemetery
With its tombstone teeth
Staggering drunkenly
Moss gathering in the tracery of long forgotten names
The melancholy unholiness
Blindly shrouded shapes
Miserably slouched and tumbled
Place me gently under a windswept sky
Where wheeling birds whistle and call
All unawares
Let the warm earth kiss and
Tenderly hold me
A mother's embrace
Let my spirit skip barelegged though tickling grasses
And nodding wildflowers
Where humble bumble bees
Tumble contently
Stumbling drunkenly
Open mouthed flowers beckoning in
Droning sleepily
Nectar drunk.

I wanted life and am given death
The promise of death
The presence of death
Death's breath on my cheek
Fetid foul, unwanted
But out of the dark, clamped tight oyster shell,
A thin sliver of light peeps out.
This is not light but love.
The promise of death has brought that gift of love.
The silver lining
The flip side
The yin and yang.
We weep.
My bald head stroked by you.

Jigsaw

I have arranged myself in my bed
My jigsaw body
My arm like a broken stick, bent at the elbow,
My hand by my head.
Fingers curled over my palm,
Furled like a flower opening.
Place a white rosebud there,
A needle of a thorn piercing the skin.
A (drop of blood) bead, a pearl of blood
Staining the blotting paper of the rose petal.
My legs folded,
Foetal
The toes, ten pebbles in a row.
The other hand on my chest.
Enclosing,
Rising and falling
Lizard tongue flicks out and licks arid, desert lips
Eyes, have to be kept open to be aware, alert.
My mind revved up
I have arranged myself (in my bed).
But inside others things are being arranged
Like dead flower in a vase
Rust brown, strange forms, alien beings
I can't even take them out

And toss them away.
The missing jigsaw piece.

Night

It is night.
The door slightly ajar
So he can hear me.
But he never does.
Instead I hear him
Moan softly.
A gentle rush of air
My heart is breaking to hear it,
Knowing
It is already broken.
I gather my words up in my hands.
A bouquet.
I hope he understands.
This is how I say I love you.

Poem?

What is a peom
Nothing at all
Or everything.
A poem is visual
There is spacing
Or breaks in a line
A line can be loong
Or
Short
It can make you laugh, cry, gasp
Or it can be boring.
It lets you say what can't be said.
The music of the soul.
One note means nothing
One word is useless
To make it sing it needs neighbours
It can be rich as a fruit cake
Every mouthful a luxury
Or
I know my pen is not dry.
I see the marks
But my head is dry
An eddy of emotions
One always bobs to the top.

Word posy

Some poems are not to share.
Some poems are only for two.
Some poems hurt too much.
Some are only for me and you.
If my poems make you cry
Then I am very sorry.
Some lovers give flowers
But
I give words.

Insomnia cure

I do not recommend poetry writing for insomnia.
It is not a sleeping pill!
Most definitely not.
Brain connections spark and sparkle electrically.
Words leap like frightened deer.
My floor is littered.
I need a garrett
I was told by the nuns, my humour is black.
Which is good as they also told me I was not funny.
I have became a strange semi-nocturnal creature.
Sitting on the toilet at two a.m. to write.
I need a net, a word net,
Or, like my dreams,
They will slip and drip between my fingers,
Water wise,
Like grainy sand on a holiday beach.
Lying in bed trying to control the chaotic, insanity, of my jumbled thoughts.
Confused by the lunatic chimes of the clock in the hall
Which make no sense at all.
This morning I am chemo tired.
My brain numb but still can't / won't settle.
My pen trembles and slurs across the page.
Chemo pen.
The words are stodgy and doughy.
Chemo words.
They came apart in my hands.

Sticky, gooey.
When I read them again I hate and despise them.
Chemo despair.

Changes

You think that if you know – you know – know.
You think that you will never say a cross word
Or be cruel
But just this morning I made a rude sign behind your back!
(You were being annoying)
You will never shout or rant or rave
(But surely you must hear me sometimes)
You will not be judgmental
You will look the other way
You will overlook
But, oh, if only things were done MY way.
You will read and travel and point and write
But my eyes are so tired.
I get panicky that I am not making a good job of this you
know – you know – know
I am not a new me after all.

Winter

The winter trees scratch the sky
Skeletal, bony, black spiky branches
The ground littered with brittle leaves
The colour of rust
Crunching like corn flakes underfoot
A puff of wind and they spiral and whirl,
In mad eddies
Tossed skyward by giddy children.
Jumped in like dry puddles.

Two halves

My world is split
Shafts of light and dark
No blurring edges
Scattered stars strewn about.
Portholes to a shimmering, shining others worldness
I step into pools of light
And feel a lightness of being.
I spread my arms and the light will lift me.
Dancing dust motes sparkle like freckles and blink.
But light can be cold, searing, fierce.
Dark is comforting
Without there is no light
The cave of my mouth.
The dark of my palm in my furled hand,
Like the heart of the unopened fronds of a fern
The surface of a pond
Shot through by the trails of tiny,
Prehistoric beasts from the darkness of time.
Plop!
The darkness of Marmite
The deep, dark, dense wisdom of my babies' eyes
Pools fringed with eyelash reeds.
The dark holds you close
Pinned mothlike.

Pancakes poems

Recipe
A poem is like a pancake
The start is not the end.
The blank page like a bowl of soft, white flour.
Unsullied, pure, white as snow.
Then the egg
Nestled in my palm
A marvel
What a feat of engineering
No seal
No door
No keyhole
No beginning no end
Shake it – silence
A mystery
A golden, smooth promise
Then brutally break the fragile shell.
The inside slides out as a gloopy whole,
Falling softly onto the flour.
Sending up puffs of white smoke eddying up
A halo of flour around the golden yolk
But like the poem, the pancake is not ready yet.
It needs to be coaxed, added to, changed.
The ideas need to be tossed.
The buttery batter becomes richly yellow.
The tasting, like the reading, will reveal all.

Night

The hospital at night
The soft shoe shuffle of the nurses
Reassuring.
My room a space pod,
Outside time and place.
I am Major Tom
All is hushed, still,
Bur for the rhythmic clicking
And gentle whirr
Of machines giving me life.
I am connected to a long, slender tube
(or is it connected to me),
Down which drips a fluid, like tears,
Entering my body.
I lie straight.
A long narrow bed.
Crisp sheets.
Starlight white
My arms folded across my chest.
As if in prayer.
My room, and I, are drifting.

Through Time and space,
I have no future
There is no past
What's outside the door

A million pinpricks of light.
My room is a womb
Gently pulsing in the belly of a whale
I glide through oceans
Happy, content, at peace.
Floating
Spinning, serenely
Gliding
All is

Cruel

My poems make you cry.
I don't mean them to.
Is it kind to be cruel.
Or cruel to be kind?

The best of times, the worst of times

A birth
A death
A wedding
A funeral
A sigh
A cry
A diagnosis
A why
A why not
A loved one crying when he thinks you can't hear.
A child stroking your face softly.
The "I love yous" texted, spoken, looked.
The knowing you wouldn't change anything.
The thought of leaving
A second chance – come and gone.
Sleepless nights – thoughts batting against the walls of your skull,
Droning like mosquitos.
The speed of life like the speed of light.
A dusting of hair off your pillow.
The kindness of people.
Known and unknown.
The cruelty of far away places.
The falling into a silent slumber like deep, soft snow.

Our souls are black and blue.
Our eyes raw
Our tears acid
Our hands held in a desperate clasp.
The bird song
Flattened
By our silent crying,
The sun blackened and charred.
The stars oddly distant
The moon and ice block.
A frozen face
My head rests on your lap
You stroke my bald head

Seagulls

When I heard the seagulls cry.
I knew I had lost you
"I love you," you whispered.
But not to me.
In the background the gulls screamed.
Scorning and mocking.
Flapping wings.
Battering the walls of my mind.
My thoughts echoed their screeching raucousness.
Layers of questions.
Layered upon layers of disbelief.
My pleas borne away.
By the wind.
As it gathered up the tattered rags of my hope.
And tossed them into the spray.
My salt tears falling into the ocean.
Standing ragged and eroded.
Ice drenched my back.
Fire burned my eyes.
I wanted you burned at the stake.
I wanted you tied to the mast.
You betrayed me.
My life is now a lie.
Only the gulls left.
Picking at the bare bones of love.
And the shipwreck of our life.

Home

I wish I could remember my mother singing to me.
But I cannot
I wish I could remember my mother saying I love you
But she did not.
Home is where you stay until you're old enough to leave.
Home is sometimes good but when it's bad it's awful.
My home is a sanctuary. A place of love, warmth and unconditional acceptance.

Dark

It's dark I feel your presence but...
Where is your love.
Where is the warmth of your lips.
Where is the heat from your loins.
You have left me in the darkness and empty.

Sun

Oh, sun on my wrinkled skin, my aching body wants life.
I am withered.
Why you ask. I say do not cry.
I drink your tears with my love.
We just embrace in the sun and cry.

Roses

The scent from the summer roses lifts my spirit.
My babies play with abandonment and joy.
They lift me higher.
I ask God to stop me dying but I know.
I am dying, quickly now, soon I will be gone
I scream.

March 2018

It's time, I must find my resting place,
No graveyard for me.
Mother earth will take me into her warm embrace.
Harsh winters and gentle summer elements will rush me to my saviour.
Into the cosmos of eternity with love and peace.

Death sentence

He, the oncologist, wanted to confirm the death sentence.
He, the oncologist didn't ask he just thought I was a number.
I stopped him.
He, the oncologist said I thought you were an intelligent woman.
How dare you I said, you the oncologist, you are without any empathy.
I said to the oncologist, go away let me live my death sentence the way I want.
And your shiny suit has stains on it.

Babies

You should see my babies.
Ava, Naomi, Zac, Gracie, Jamie, William.
They are divine. God why do I have to leave my joy?
The cancer will take me from my babies but not yet.
I will cuddle them, read to them, make them laugh.
They give me life they are precious.
Oh babies, try to remember me. I love you. I loved you.
I will always be with you, just look up and think of me a little.
All my love
xxxxxx

Morphine

There are moments when the precious morphine abates.
The pain screams out, but I am alive.
Oh, my beloved I can see the agony in your eyes, yes, I am going.
I give you my life, take it. I lived for you, that is all I could do.
All I wanted
Hold my wretched body close, kiss my dry lips, stroke me, I am drifting away.
Morphine is taking me.
Oh, my love, my love, my love,
I…

Mike

Hi Mike, did you know you left me for far too long.
And now I haven't got long for living.
Do you remember I was beautiful, at least I thought I was, did you?
Why did you always have to leave me for so long.
You said you adored me but not enough to give me more of your body,
To take me higher.
I was lonely, didn't you know?
My babies saved me, my grandchildren and the babies of others.
They loved me unconditionally, whisper in my ear that you did.
I haven't got much time.
You did love me unconditionally, I know.
Mike, I love you.

What Am I

Do you know what I am?
I try to recall but the pain takes me.
Tell me my love, tell me what I am.
You said I was beautiful, am I now?
I don't think I am.
You said I was intelligent and funny, am I now?
You said I thrilled you, that you wanted me, do you want me now?
What am I, tell me my love, am I still your Maggie, your brown eyed girl.
I need to know what I am?

Magda

My relief when you come Magda to give me my morphine,
so gentle.
My pain melts, your beautiful Polish voice, the warmth of
your words, you know my needs.
Be with me if you can
As I slip away, make it gentle
I pray for you Magda and give thanks for you,
my angel of mercy.

Praise of Nigeria

Nigeria has given me my beautiful doctor.
She sparkles with beauty, glamour and hope.
She knows I am a glamour queen in a disguise.
Time for us to be feminine, time to laugh at husbands and lovers.
To dream of freedom from anxiety, free from pain.
We exchange words of meaning woman to woman,
my beautiful
Nigerian doctor blesses me with her warmth as she hugs me.
Does she know that I will pass soon?

The hill

March 2016 a time to choose my resting place on earth.
You hold me tight as we climb. I am cold to my being,
frozen as the snow melts on my thin face.
Little steps you say
The keeper of dead bodies smiled as he sees us, not long for
this beautiful world. I know he wants me.
I raise my head and see the distant snow-covered hills and
the keeper of dead bodies willing me to concede to early
death.
I will not, I want time.

With you

Many years from now I'll still be with those whom I held dear. I'll be sitting in the garden, listening to loved ones talk.
I'll be admiring the view with them on long walks as the sunlight paints the hill gold.
I'll be laughing at your jokes and longing to hear how your day was.
I'll be by their side as they walk through their lives.
I'll be there to see children grow older, triumphs, disasters, marriages, births, and yes, death to.
Still in the same book, not far away at all, just on a different page.